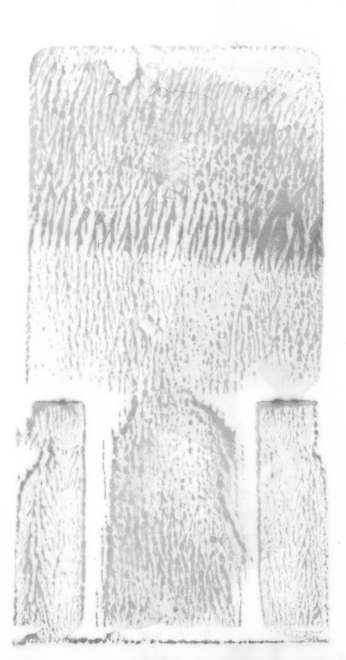

music

for

keyboard

harmony

PRENTICE-HALL INTERNATIONAL, INC., *London*
PRENTICE-HALL OF AUSTRALIA, PTY., LTD., *Sydney*
PRENTICE-HALL OF CANADA, LTD., *Toronto*
PRENTICE-HALL OF INDIA (PRIVATE) LTD., *New Delhi*
PRENTICE-HALL OF JAPAN, INC., *Tokyo*

music
for
keyboard
harmony

ROBERT A. MELCHER
Professor of Music Theory, Conservatory of Music, Oberlin College

WILLARD WARCH
Associate Professor of Music Theory, Conservatory of Music, Oberlin College

PRENTICE-HALL, INC., Englewood Cliffs, New Jersey

CONTENTS

INTRODUCTION

The purpose of this book is to provide material for various kinds of keyboard training in classes of Music Theory and Functional Piano. Each chapter contains a brief discussion of the new vocabulary and music for various kinds of application to these chords.

The material is arranged in order of progressive difficulty to follow the normal sequence of the student's growing harmonic vocabulary. It is arranged in accordance with general teaching practice rather than in agreement with any specific harmony text. Therefore, it can be used with a variety of harmony books and teaching situations. In addition, the material need not always be presented in the order in which it appears in this book. Modulation, for instance, may be introduced much earlier if the teacher so desires.

Three types of music are included in this volume:

1. MELODIES TO BE ACCOMPANIED IN A PIANO STYLE

A most important and helpful feature is that each chapter gives assignments that can be worked out on three levels of difficulty:

A. For the beginning pianist the accompaniments to be played in the two hands while the melody is played by another student either at a second piano or at the same piano one or two octaves higher than printed.

B. For the intermediate pianist the accompaniments to be played in a simple style by the left hand while the melody is played by the right hand.

C. For the fluent pianist the accompaniments and styles may be as elaborate as the student can manage.

2. CONTINUO PARTS

These are to be "realized" from figured basses. Drawn chiefly from the literature of the late Baroque period, they may be harmonized almost exclusively in four-part style or they may be elaborated in various manners characteristic of that era. This book, however, makes no attempt to present the various niceties and details of continuo realization as practiced in the Baroque period. Rather, the purpose is to teach the student, in musical settings, the basic principles of chord connections and to provide him with a solid basis for advanced study in this area if he should choose to pursue it further.

It is an enjoyable and valuable experience to have the solo parts of the continuo excerpts performed by class members who are singers, violinists, or players of treble-clef woodwind or brass instruments. If such performers are not available in the class, these solo parts may be played either at a second piano or at the same piano an octave higher. Ideally, accompaniments should be played on the harpsichord or organ, with a cello doubling the bass line; but a discreet performance at the piano, with or without cello, is also satisfactory.

The earlier chapters contain short figured basses to be played in four-part harmony as preparation for the continuo excerpts.

3. IMPROVISATION

This is to be done (1) by improvising over given harmonic patterns and (2) by continuing given beginnings into various forms. Vocabulary becomes a student's own only as he uses it to express his own musical ideas. Originality and imagination can and should be stimulated and guided into artistic musical speech.

FUNCTIONAL PIANO

Students in Functional Piano classes must be able to use basic chords fluently. To attain this goal, the teacher may prefer to concentrate upon acquiring a vocabulary of various accompaniment styles, accompanying the printed familiar melodies (both folk and composed), accompanying by ear the melodies listed by title only, and various kinds of improvising. The more detailed study of the realization of continuos may be left to the theory class.

In order to keep this book to a practical length, the authors have intentionally omitted certain aspects of keyboard training, such as:

1. Basic fundamentals: scales, arpeggios, intervals, etc.

   It is assumed that students will possess such knowledge before beginning this book. If they do not, the teacher can easily make such assignments as the needs of the students require.

2. Sight playing and transposition

   The inclusion of enough material to develop real skill in these areas would make this volume far too large, but it is recommended that students transpose many of the examples, continuos, and melodies with their accompaniments to other keys.

3. Score reading

   If the teacher wishes to include this skill in the course, he may use any of the available books devoted to this topic, or open scores of choral music, string quartets, symphonies, etc.

However, this book does contain more material than most classes can use. Whatever is not used at the keyboard may be used as written assignments. In this way the book may serve as a substitute for a theory text.

Many of the melodies are excellent for sight singing, and any of the material can well be used for dictation practice. It is strongly urged that after the students have worked out their own accompaniments to the composed melodies, the teacher play the passages on the piano or the phonograph, and the class find by ear the composer's own harmonies and accompaniment style.

Imaginative teachers will find a variety of uses for the music in this book, and the teacher is always to be free to use it in any way that best fits the needs of his students rather than to restrict himself only to the suggestions given in the book.

Robert A. Melcher
Willard Warch

music

for

keyboard

harmony

Chapter One

THE TONIC AND DOMINANT CHORDS

Once started, any piece of music is a movement toward a goal or point of rest. The point of departure may vary, but the goal of most harmonic music is its tonic.

The chord most frequently used to carry a composition to its goal is the one built on the fifth or dominant degree of the scale. Tonic and dominant chords can be arranged in many ways. The simplest arrangement, however, is for four voices that might be sung by four people or played on four instruments. This version also fits easily under the fingers of a pianist.

EXAMPLE 1. *

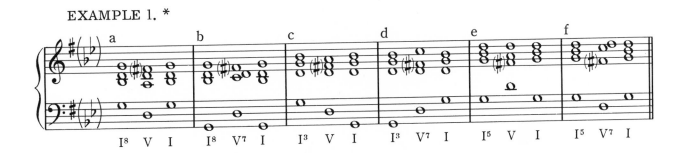

Observe in Example 1 that:

1. The root, third, or fifth may be at the top of the chord. The Arabic figure (8, 3, or 5) beside the first Roman numeral I indicates which member is in the top voice of the first chord.

2. The bass voice is doubled.

3. When the seventh is used in the dominant chord, the fifth is omitted.

4. A tone common to two successive chords is kept in the same voice.

5. The remaining upper two voices always move stepwise to the nearest chord members.

*In this and many subsequent examples two signatures are given to show that the progressions can be done in both major and minor modes.

1

Assignment 1. Play the above progressions in all keys, using the same fingerings at all times in all keys. Be able to write the progressions from memory in any key.

VOICE LEADING

Divide the class into sopranos, altos, tenors, and basses; sing the chords of Example 1. Notice that each voice moves independently, that is, differently from the other three; that the voice which has the leading tone (the seventh degree of the scale, which is also the third of the dominant chord) has a pull or desire to return to the tonic, while the voice which has the subdominant (the fourth degree of the scale, the seventh of the V_7) wants to resolve down to the third of the tonic chord. Test this by having the basses move on to the final chord while the other voices hold their V_7 tones and then resolve them. Notice also that the voice which has the fifth of the tonic chord keeps the same tone in both chords.

Assignment 2. Sing in four parts the progressions of Example 1 in various major and minor keys.

FIGURED BASSES

When the bass is given, the pianist can easily supply the upper three voices of the chords. In the following basses, the Arabic number under the first note indicates the top voice for the first chord. When the bass repeats itself, you may change the position of the other three voices for the sake of interest. Observe that all of the progressions do not start on the tonic chord. These chords may be considered as an accompaniment with the melody missing.

Example 2 shows two ways in which the first of the following basses may be harmonized.

EXAMPLE 2.

Play the following progressions in four-part harmony. Also begin some of them with soprano notes other than those indicated.

PIANO ACCOMPANIMENT PATTERNS

The chords of Example 1 may be played as "after beats" in the right hand to accompany a melody sung or played by another person.

EXAMPLE 3.

J. J. Rousseau, *Le Rêve*

The following are common rhythmic patterns for "after beats"
in various meters:

EXAMPLE 4.

The left hand may play the entire accompaniment while the right hand
plays the melody.

EXAMPLE 5.

Schubert, *Ländler No. 3, Op. 18*
(Original in A♭)

For the less skillful pianists, the accompaniment may be arranged in a simpler fashion, making it possible to keep the left hand in a position directly over the notes it plays.*

EXAMPLE 6.

Allegro moderato   Polish

Assignment 4.   Play accompaniments to the following melodies in the various styles that have been suggested.

Allegro gioviale   Swedish

1.

*For patterns that lie even more easily under the left hand, see Chapter 5, Example 1 and 6.

5

*Accompany with V_7. In these lessons the ninth of V_9 will be used in the melody only.

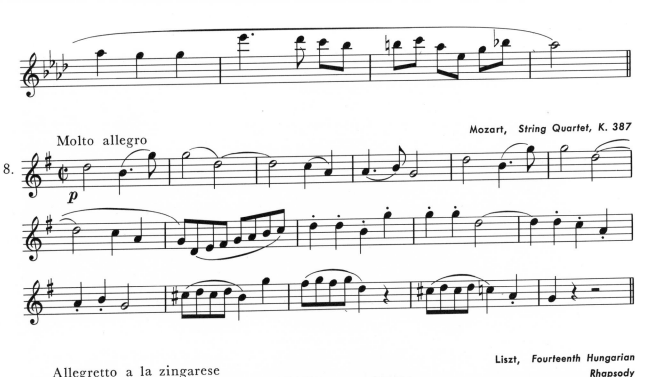

8. **Molto allegro**

Mozart, *String Quartet, K. 387*

p

9. **Allegretto a la zingarese**

Liszt, *Fourteenth Hungarian Rhapsody*

dolce con grazia

10. **Allegro**

Beethoven, *String Trio, Op. 3*

dolce

11. **Molto vivace**

Chopin, *Waltz in G♭ major, Op. 70, No. 1*

f *tr* *8va*

Assignment 5.   Play by ear accompaniments to the following familiar songs:

1. Ach du Lieber Augustin (Did You Ever See a Lassie?)
2. Alouette
3. Down in the Valley
4. The Farmer in the Dell
5. Hail, Hail, the Gang's All Here
6. Here We Go Round the Mulberry Bush
7. The Irish Washerwoman
8. Lightly Row
9. London Bridge
10. Long, Long Ago
11. Looby Loo
12. Merrily We Roll Along
13. Mexican Hat Dance
14. Oats and Beans and Barley Grow
15. Oh Dear, What Can the Matter Be?
16. Oh Where, Oh Where Has My Little Dog Gone?
17. Polly Wolly Doodle
18. Shoo Fly
19. Skip to My Lou
20. Sing a Song of Sixpence
21. Susie, Little Susie
22. Three Blind Mice

ALBERTI BASS

The "after-beat" is not the only style of accompaniment; indeed, it is not appropriate for all melodies. Some melodies sound well when played with the so-called <u>Alberti bass</u>, which is characteristic of much of the keyboard music of Haydn, Mozart, and their precursors. In this broken-chord style of accompaniment, the seventh of the dominant may ascend to the fifth of the tonic in the course of a phrase, but at a final cadence it must descend to the third of the tonic.

EXAMPLE 7.

9

In $\frac{3}{4}$ and $\frac{6}{8}$ meters the Alberti accompaniment patterns may be arranged thus.

EXAMPLE 8.

Assignment 6.   Accompany melodies 1, 2, 4, and 10 of Assignment 4 in this
style.
Accompany others for which you think the Alberti style
is appropriate.

OTHER STYLES

The following are simple variants of the "after beat" which may more
effectively portray the character of a given melody:

EXAMPLE 9.

Assignment 7. Use some of the styles suggested in Example 9 to accompany those melodies on pages 5-8 for which you think they would be appropriate.

Assignment 8. Some of the styles given in Example 9 are often employed in lullabies to suggest the rocking of a cradle. The following are two well-known lullabies; accompany them in their entirety in the styles used by their composers.

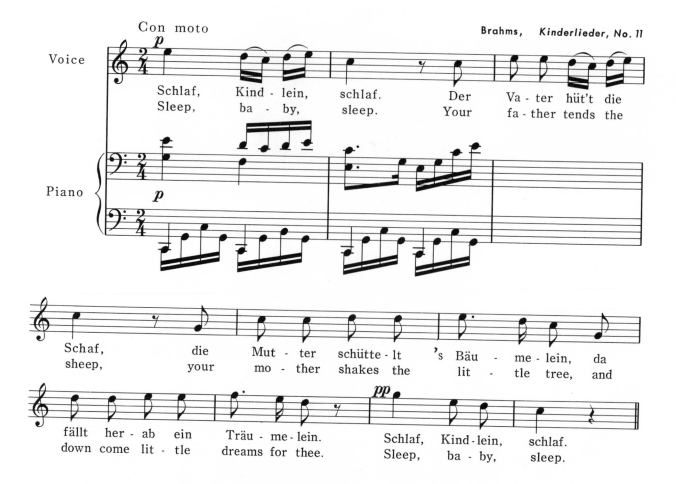

Con moto

Voice

Schlaf, Kind - lein, schlaf. Der Va - ter hüt't die
Sleep, ba - by, sleep. Your fa - ther tends the

Piano

Schaf, die Mut - ter schütte - lt 's Bäu - me - lein, da
sheep, your mo - ther shakes the lit - tle tree, and

fällt her - ab ein Träu - me - lein. Schlaf, Kind - lein, schlaf.
down come lit - tle dreams for thee. Sleep, ba - by, sleep.

Assignment 9. Accompany some of the other melodies on pages 5-8 in styles that seem appropriate to you. Do not limit yourself to the styles suggested thus far, but let your imagination suggest other ways of providing appropriate accompaniment patterns.

IMPROVISATION

Improvising is not a matter of aimless meandering, but should always be a carefully controlled procedure. The following four steps provide one simple way to begin to learn to improvise: 1) Decide upon a harmonic pattern of two four-measure phrases; 2) Select a key, meter, tempo, and style of accompaniment pattern; 3) Above this accompaniment, add a very simple melody of one note for each chord, the first phrase ending with some feeling of incompleteness and the second with a feeling of finality. This form is called a period; 4) Elaborate this basic melody.

A possible solution to the above steps might be:

1. Harmonic pattern: I | I | V | I | V | I | V | I ‖

2. Key, meter, tempo, accompaniment style:

Andantino   or

3. Simple melody of one note to each chord:

4. Melody of No. 3. elaborated:

Assignment 10. Following the four-step process given above, improvise in various styles to the following harmonic patterns. In some cases play only the bass line in the left hand and the harmonies in the right hand while you spontaneously sing a melody or another person plays a melody that will fit these chords; in other cases, play the accompaniment in the left hand and improvise a melody in the right hand. Employ different meters and tempi; do some in the minor mode as well as in the major. Add the seventh to the dominant chord where it seems appropriate.

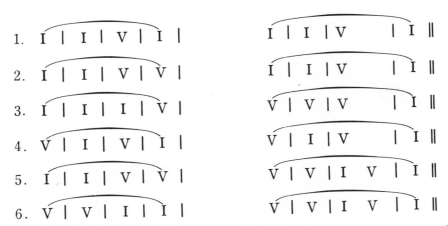

1. I | I | V | I | I | I | V | I ‖
2. I | I | V | V | I | I | V | I ‖
3. I | I | I | V | V | V | V | I ‖
4. V | I | V | I | V | I | V | I ‖
5. I | I | V | V | V | V | I V | I ‖
6. V | V | I | I | V | V | I V | I ‖

13

Chapter Two

THE SUBDOMINANT TRIAD

Triads built on the first, fourth, and fifth degrees of a major or minor scale contain among them all the tones of that scale, and therefore allow us to treat any note of a diatonic melody as a chord tone. These three chords, tonic (I), subdominant (IV), and dominant (V) are known as the primary triads.

In the progression I IV I the common tone is kept in the same voice. But in going from IV to V the upper three voices must move in contrary motion to the bass because there is no common tone between these two chords. In going from IV to V_7 in the simplest procedure, the upper voice which has the doubled root of IV remains as the common tone, becoming the seventh of V_7, and the fifth must be omitted from the dominant.

EXAMPLE 1.

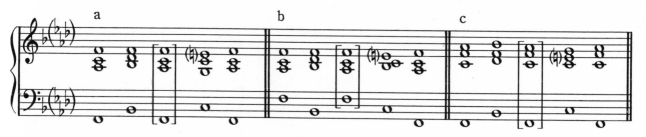

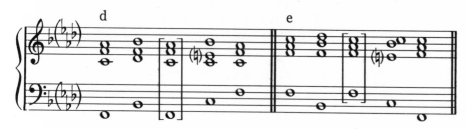

Assignment 1. Play the progressions in Example 1 in all three positions and in all keys, first with, then omitting the bracketed tonic chord. Sing these progressions in four parts in various major and minor keys.

FIGURED BASSES

Assignment 2. Play the following figured basses in four-part style. Then begin some of them with soprano notes other than those indicated.

14

CONTINUO

In the seventeenth and eighteenth centuries, accompaniments to both solo and ensemble music were customarily played ("realized") on a keyboard instrument (harpsichord or organ) from a single bass line with figures giving the necessary information as to what the upper voices of the accompaniment should be. This keyboard accompaniment part was called the continuo and was in addition to the melody and parts being performed by the soloists or orchestra. Because the bass of the eighteenth-century harpsichord was not loud and sustained enough to make a satisfactory balance, the bass line was customarily doubled by a cello.

The left hand plays the given bass line and the right hand plays the remaining three voices to complete the four-part harmony, just as in the playing of figured basses.

Example 2 shows two ways in which the first of the following continuos may be "realized."

EXAMPLE 2.

Assignment 3.   "Realize" the following continuo basses in four-part style.
The solo lines should be performed by class members or
played on another piano.

*For the original version of this phrase, see Chapter 5, Assignment 6, number
2.

2.** Allegro

3. Moderato

**This and all other excerpts in Assignment 3 are duets with continuo accompaniment. The accompanist plays neither of the violin parts, but only the continuo bass in the left hand and the "realization" in the right hand.

18

"After beats" involving the chord of IV pose no new problem. They are merely an elaboration of the four-part progressions, as shown in Example 3:

EXAMPLE 3.

Assignment 4.   Play the accompaniment to the above melody using the chords in the other two positions. Elementary pianists may play the bass notes in the left hand and the "after beats" in the right hand, while another student plays or sings the melody.

The principles of four-part writing may also be followed in varying the "after beats."

EXAMPLE 4.

19

Play the chords of Example 1 in the style of "after beats" and its variants. Adapt some of the variants shown in Chapter 1, Example 9 to this harmonic pattern.

ALBERTI BASS

If root position triads are connected thus,

reducing the chords to their block forms

creates consecutive perfect fifths which are not used in this style. To avoid this objectionable voice leading, omit the fifth and double the root in the <u>lower</u> of the two triads.

EXAMPLE 5.

When we apply this principle to the German folk song of Example 3, the Alberti accompaniment will be as follows:*

*For a pattern that lies more easily under the left hand, see Chapter 5, Example 3 a and b.

The third measure of the alternate version shows the presence of the fifth with the third omitted in the left hand. This is good here because of the prominence of the third in the melody.

This same rule (omit the fifth and double the root of the lower of the triads) applies when small chords are used for accompaniments in the "after beat" style.

EXAMPLE 6.

Assignment 6.   Accompany the following melodies in the styles which you consider appropriate, following the principles presented thus far. See Chapter 1, Examples 4, 7, 8, and 9.

FAMILIAR SONGS

12.

13.

14.

15.

Assignment 7. Below is another well-known lullaby. Accompany it in the style the composer has used.

Brahms, *Wiegenlied, Op. 49, No. 4*

Gut-en A - bend, gut' Nacht, mit
Lul - la - by and good night, with

Ro - sen be - dacht, mit Näg-lein be - steckt schlupf' un - ter die
ro - ses be - dight, with li - lies o'er - spread is Ba - by's wee

Deck'; mor - gen früh wenn Gott will, wirst du wie - der ge -
bed; Lay thee down now and rest, may thy slum - ber be

weckt, mor - gen früh wenn Gott will, wirst du wie - der ge - weckt.
blest, lay thee down now and rest, may thy slum - ber be blest.

Play by ear accompaniments to the following familiar songs:

1. Aloha Oe (chorus)
2. Aunt Dinah's Quilting Party
3. For He's a Jolly Good Fellow
4. Hickory Dickory Dock
5. Home, Sweet Home
6. Juanita
7. The Marines' Hymn
8. Old McDonald Had a Farm
9. Red River Valley
10. Tramp, Tramp, Tramp, the Boys Are Marching

IMPROVISATION

Improvisation including the subdominant triad may follow the four-step process presented in Chapter 1, page 12-13.

1. Harmonic pattern:

2. Key, meter, tempo, accompaniment style:

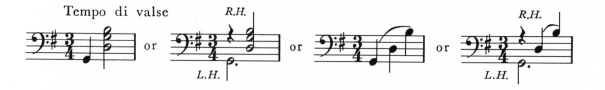

3. Simple melody of one note to each chord:

4. Melody of No. 3 elaborated:

Further elaborations of this basic melody might be:

Assignment 9. Using the above four-step process, improvise melodies and accompaniments over the following harmonic patterns. Employ various styles, keys, and meters. Add the seventh to the dominant chord where it seems appropriate.

1. I | I | IV | I | I | I | V | I ||
2. I | IV | I | V | I | IV | V | I ||
3. I | I | IV | V | I | I | IV   V | I ||
4. V | I | V | I | IV | IV | V | I ||
5. IV | V | I | V | I   V | I   IV | V | I ||
6. I | V | I | V | IV | I | V | I ||

Chapter Three

THE CADENTIAL TONIC SIX-FOUR CHORD

The following much-used cadential formula

EXAMPLE 1.

has been modified or varied in many ways. One of the most common variants is

EXAMPLE 2.

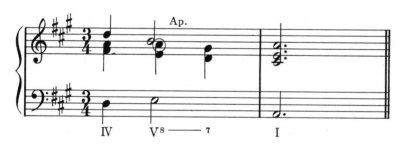

Another variant is

EXAMPLE 3.

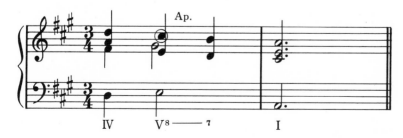

The variant which is most often found uses two appoggiaturas.

EXAMPLE 4.

However, when this cadence is found in a more elaborate version, such as

EXAMPLE 5.

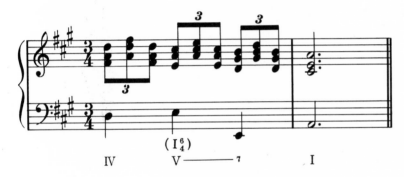

it is no longer so apparent that the second chord is a dominant triad with two appoggiaturas. Because the notes of the chord on the second beat spell a tonic triad with the fifth in the bass, it is commonly labeled I $\frac{6}{4}$. Beat two, nonetheless, has dominant function. When a tonic six-four is followed by a dominant chord, the I $\frac{6}{4}$ will be heard as a dominant, and a musical use of the six-four will be one that takes this into account.

The most common use of I $\frac{6}{4}$ is at a cadence. Here it must come on a beat, or part of a beat, which is rhythmically stronger than the dominant chord to which it resolves.

EXAMPLE 6.

Observe that when the I $^6_4$ has the third in the top voice, it is commonly followed by a complete V$_7$. Any position of the chord may, of course, be followed by either a complete or incomplete V$_7$.

EXAMPLE 7.

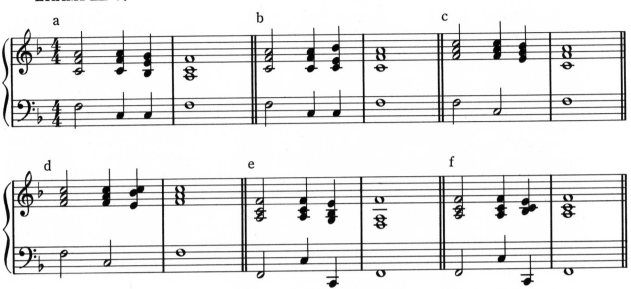

Because the cadential I $^6_4$ is dominant in function, it should be preceded by a chord of tonic or subdominant function.

EXAMPLE 8.

To precede the cadential I $\begin{smallmatrix} 6 \\ 4 \end{smallmatrix}$ with a dominant chord makes it relatively weak and ineffective.

EXAMPLE 9.

If one changes the meter of Example 9 to $\begin{smallmatrix} 3 \\ 8 \end{smallmatrix}$, the entire second measure becomes dominant, with the C-sharp and A on the second beat being passing tones. This second beat is, therefore, not a cadential I $\begin{smallmatrix} 6 \\ 4 \end{smallmatrix}$.

EXAMPLE 10.

The symbols T, S, and D above Examples 8, 9, and 10 refer to the tonic, subdominant, or dominant function of the chords under them.

Assignment 1. Play the progressions in Examples 6 and 7 in other keys, and in both the major and minor modes.

FIGURED BASSES AND CONTINUOS

Assignment 2. Play the following figured basses in four-part style. For the rest of this book, the position of the first chord will not be given. The progressions may be played from any or all positions. Two or more successive figures under the same bass note (even though the note may be repeated or leap an octave) show voice leading in the same voice or part. Thus, $\begin{smallmatrix} 6 \\ 4 \end{smallmatrix}$ $\begin{smallmatrix} 5 \\ 3 \end{smallmatrix}$ indicate that one voice moves from a sixth to a fifth above the bass while another voice moves from a fourth to a third.

32

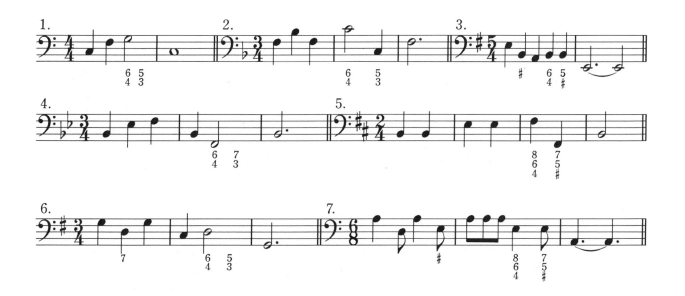

Assignment 3. Realize the following continuos.

PIANO ACCOMPANIMENTS

When used to accompany melodies in piano style, the cadential I $\frac{6}{4}$ chord usually presents no new problems. There are, however, certain situations which demand special solutions, some of which are shown in Example 11.

EXAMPLE 11.

Assignment 4.   Accompany the following melodies in appropriate styles.

Andante   Mozart, Trio, K. 498

10.

Assignment 5.   Play by ear accompaniments to the following familiar songs:

1.   Believe Me If All Those Endearing Young Charms
2.   The Farmer in the Dell
3.   Goodnight, Ladies
4.   Li'l Liza Jane
5.   Oh! Susanna
6.   Old Folks at Home
7.   Silent Night
8.   Yankee Doodle
9.   You Are My Sunshine

Chapter Four

THE SUPERTONIC TRIAD

In Example 1 the melody of the second measure may be harmonized in two slightly different ways. Note that in the second version of the left hand one note is different—the subdominant chord has E instead of D.

EXAMPLE 1.

Although the two chords are much alike in effect, there <u>is</u> a difference. Version two uses the first inversion of the supertonic chord (II_6), a minor triad (E G B), instead of IV in root position, a major triad (G B D). The supertonic sixth (II_6) as used here is obviously a substitute for IV, though when one considers that many composers (Mozart for one) used II_6 in the cadence much more frequently than IV, it becomes questionable as to which is the basic subdominant and which is the substitute.

FURTHER CONSIDERATIONS

1. The II_6 allows us to harmonize the second degree of the scale in the melody as a subdominant.

2. Playing Example 1 in the minor mode shows that IV in minor is a minor triad and II_6 is a diminished triad.

3. In eighteenth-and nineteenth-century music, the supertonic chord was used more frequently in the first inversion than in root position.

<u>Assignment 1.</u>   Play the following in other keys in both the major and minor modes. Then play them omitting the I $^6_4$ chords.

EXAMPLE 2.

FIGURED BASSES

Assignment 2. Harmonize the following figured basses. Avoid having the fifth of II or II$_6$ in the soprano, and resolve II or II$_6$ to I$^6_4$ or V by moving the upper three voices downward to the nearest chord tones.

CONTINUOS

In the Baroque period the cadential I $\begin{smallmatrix}6\\4\end{smallmatrix}$ was not used as frequently as was the dominant chord with the entrance of the third delayed by an appoggiatura (usually prepared). The Arabic figures 4 3 indicate this voice leading. Examples 3 a and b illustrate this principle, as well as the use of I$_6$.

EXAMPLE 3.

Assignment 3. Realize the following continuos.

2. Presto — Flute, Violin, Cembalo — Telemann, *Suite in B minor*

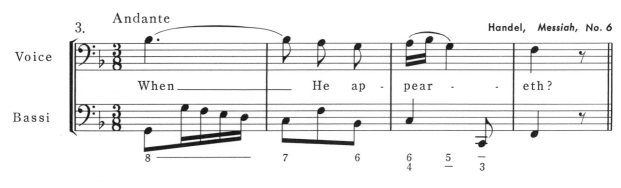

3. Andante — Voice, Bassi — Handel, *Messiah, No. 6*

When _____ He ap - pear - - eth?

4. Violins I/II, Cembalo — Corelli, *Sonata, Op. 3, No. 10*

①

② See Willi Apel, "Corelli Clash," <u>Harvard Dictionary of Music</u> (Cambridge, Mass. Harvard University Press, 1944).

② See Apel, "Hemiola," <u>Harvard Dictionary of Music</u>.

Handel, Concerto Grosso, Op. 6, No. 1

PIANO ACCOMPANIMENTS

<u>Assignment 4.</u>　Accompany the following melodies in appropriate styles.

FAMILIAR SONGS

Assignment 5. Play by ear accompaniments to the following familiar songs:

1. Away in a Manger
2. Battle Hymn of the Republic
3. Bobby Shafto
4. Dark Eyes
5. The Glow Worm
6. Happy Birthday
7. Little Jack Horner
8. The Muffin Man
9. My Bonnie
10. Oh, Dem Golden Slippers
11. O Sole Mio
12. Santa Lucia
13. Two Guitars

Assignment 6. Continue the accompaniments to the following melodies in the styles used by the composers.

IMPROVISATION

Assignment 7.   Improvise in various styles, keys, and meters over the following harmonic patterns.

1. I | II₆ | V | I | I | II₆ | V₇ | I ‖

$$\text{1.} \quad \text{I} \mid \text{II}_6 \mid \text{V} \mid \text{I} \quad \mid \text{I} \mid \text{II}_6 \mid \text{V}_7 \mid \text{I} \;\|$$

$$\text{2.} \quad \text{I} \mid \text{IV} \mid \text{I} \mid \text{I}_4^6 \; \text{V} \quad \mid \text{I} \mid \text{II}_6 \mid \text{I}_4^6 \; \text{V}_7 \mid \text{I} \;\|$$

$$\text{3.} \quad \text{V}_7 \mid \text{I} \mid \text{II}_6 \mid \text{V} \quad \mid \text{V}_7 \mid \text{I} \mid \text{II}_6 \; \text{V}_7 \mid \text{I} \;\|$$

$$\text{4.} \quad \text{I} \mid \text{IV} \mid \text{II} \mid \text{V} \quad \mid \text{IV} \mid \text{II} \mid \text{I}_4^6 \; \text{V}_7 \mid \text{I} \;\|$$

$$\text{5.} \quad \text{I} \; \text{V}_7 \mid \text{I} \mid \text{IV} \; \text{II} \mid \text{I}_4^6 \; \text{V} \quad \mid \text{I} \; \text{V}_7 \mid \text{I} \; \text{II}_6 \mid \text{I}_4^6 \; \text{V}_7 \mid \text{I} \;\|$$

$$\text{6.} \quad \text{I} \mid \text{V} \mid \text{I} \mid \text{II}_6 \; \text{V} \quad \mid \text{I} \mid \text{IV} \; \text{II}_6 \mid \text{I}_4^6 \; \text{V}_7 \mid \text{I} \;\|$$

Chapter Five

INVERSIONS OF I, IV, V, AND V₇

It is said that when Brahms examined a song brought to him by a student, he would first cover the treble staff of the accompaniment and focus his attention on the vocal melody and the bass line of the accompaniment as the two most important elements in the music. Certainly, before the bass of a composition can lay claim to distinction, much less to being a sort of "bass melody," it is necessary for it to include chord inversions in its line.

NEIGHBORING MOTION

Inversions are frequently used as "neighboring chords," in which the bass line moves stepwise around the basic harmonies. The melody in Chapter 1, Example 3, might well be harmonized thus:

EXAMPLE 1.

J. J. Rousseau, *Le Rêve*

A reduction of the melody and bass line to their basic structure makes apparent the neighboring function of V_5^6 in the third measure and V_6 in the fifth measure.

EXAMPLE 2.

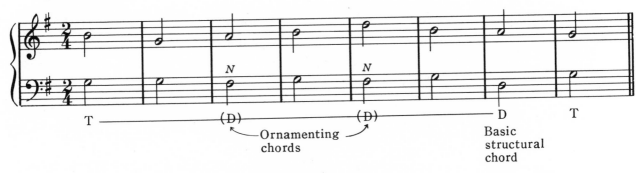

The IV$_4^6$ between two tonic chords in root position provides another example of neighbor motion. The first four measures of the melody of Chapter 2, Example 3, could be harmonized thus:

EXAMPLE 3.

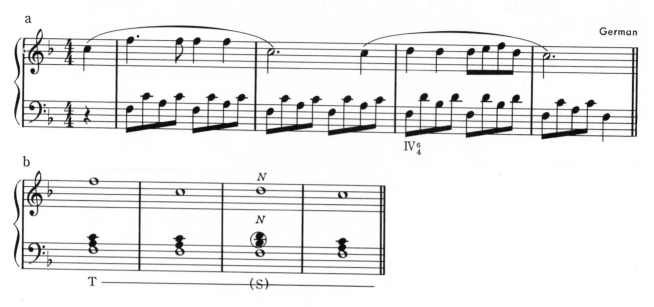

If IV$_6$ be used in the third measure, it, too, acts as a neighboring chord.

EXAMPLE 4.

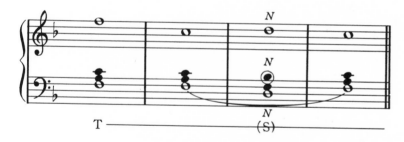

Many theorists today would also consider the root position IV used in the original harmonization of this phrase to be an ornamenting neighbor chord.

Inversions of the V$_7$ chord often function as neighbor motion, as shown in Example 5, which is the last four measures of Example 3. The I$_6$ in the third measure from the end provides a more interesting approach to II$_6$, a more colorful chord than IV.

EXAMPLE 5.

Example 6 shows another use of neighbor motion, often called "double neighbor," in which the bass moves on each side of the note it ornaments instead of returning directly to it.

EXAMPLE 6.

Donizetti, *Lucrezia Borgia,*
Act 1, No. 3

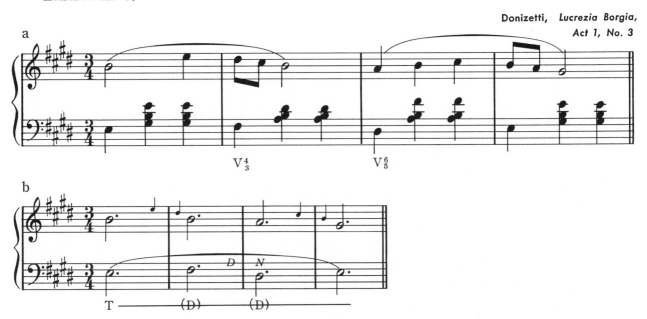

The following four-part progressions illustrate common uses of chords as neighbor motion.

EXAMPLE 7.

Assignment 1.   Play the progressions in Example 7 in other keys, both major and minor. Also play them from other positions of the first tonic chord.

Assignment 2. Accompany the following melodies, which have already been harmonized in simpler versions, but which can now be made more interesting by employing the principles presented above:

Chapter 1, Assignment 4, Nos. 1, 2, 3, 4, 10.

Chapter 2, Assignment 6, Nos. 1, 2, 3, 8.

Chapter 3, Assignment 4, Nos. 1, 6.

Chapter 4, Assignment 4, No. 4.

PASSING MOTION

Inversions often function as "passing chords" between root positions of two different chords.

EXAMPLE 8.

The V_4^6 and V_3^4 chords often supply passing motion between I and I_6.

EXAMPLE 9.

The $_4^6$ inversion may also be used as motion within the same chord. Here the second inversion of the triad always comes on a relatively unaccented beat.

EXAMPLE 10.

A similar use of this chord is frequently found in waltzes and marches.

EXAMPLE 11.

The following four-part progressions illustrate common uses of chords as passing motion.

EXAMPLE 12.

Assignment 3. Play the progressions in Example 12 in other keys, both major and minor. Also play them from other positions of the first tonic chord.

Assignment 4. Accompany the following melodies, employing the principles of both passing and neighboring motion:

Chapter 1, Assignment 4, Nos. 6, 7, 8, 9.

Chapter 2, Assignment 6, Nos. 4, 5, 6, 7, 10.

Chapter 3, Assignment 4, Nos. 2, 5, 7, 8.

Chapter 4, Assignment 4, Nos. 1, 2, 3, 5, 8.

Assignment 5. Harmonize the following figured basses in four-part style.

Assignment 6. Realize the following continuos.

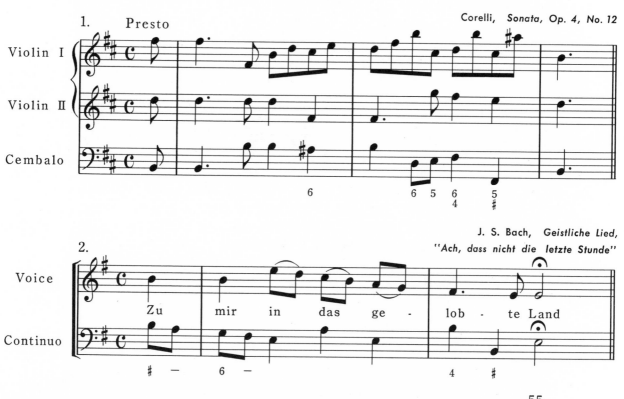

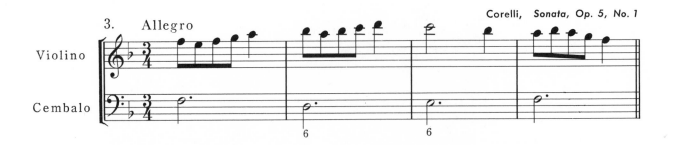

3. Allegro — Corelli, *Sonata, Op. 5, No. 1* — Violino / Cembalo

4. Presto — Telemann, *Suite in E major* — Flute / Violin / Cembalo

5. Tempo di Giga — Corelli, *Sonata, Op. 4, No. 12* — Violin I / Violin II / Organo

6. Menuet — Telemann, *Suite in B♭ major* — Flute / Violin / Continuo

ALBERTI BASS

Inversions lend themselves well to Alberti accompaniments, for the figurations lie easily under the left hand. In this style (as in all styles of accompaniments), the melody and bass should be independent voices, with the bass making a good counterpoint to the simplified structure of the melody.

EXAMPLE 13.

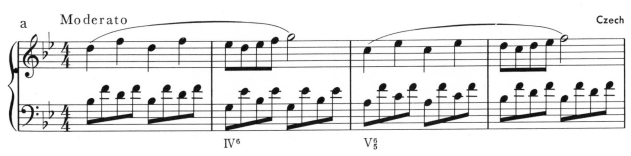

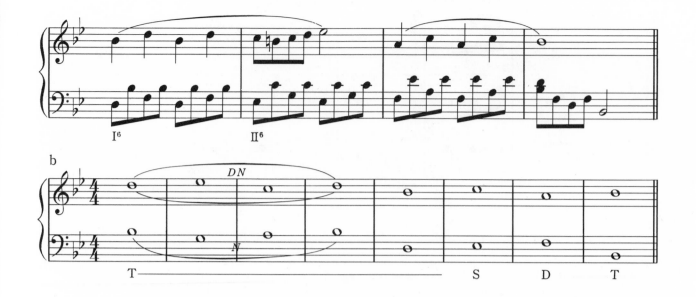

In an Alberti bass, the V_7 root-position chord in the left hand must omit either the third or the fifth, depending on which note is more prominent in the melody. Thus, if in the seventh measure of Example 13, the melody had been more predominantly the leading tone, the left hand pattern would have omitted the third.

EXAMPLE 14.

Assignment 7. Accompany each of the following melodies with an Alberti bass.

Beethoven, *String Trio,*
Op. 3 (Adapted)

IMPROVISATION

Harmonic Patterns

Assignment 8.   Over the following harmonic patterns, play Alberti accompaniments in the left hand and a melody in the right hand. Use various keys, both major and minor.

1. $\frac{4}{4}$ | I | V_3^4 | V_5^6 | I | IV_4^6 | I I_6 | II_6 V | I ‖

2. $\frac{6}{8}$ | I | V_6 | I IV_6 | I_4^6 V | V_2 | I_6 II_6 | I_4^6 V_7 | I ‖

3. $\frac{4}{4}$ | I I_6 | IV I_6 | V_3^4 I | I_4^6 V_{-2} | I_6 V_3^4 | I_6 II_6 | I_4^6 V | I ‖

4. $\frac{6}{8}$ | I I_6 | IV V_2 | I_6 II_6 | I_4^6 V | I_6 I | I_4^6 I_6 | II_6 V_7 | I ‖

5. $\frac{3}{4}$ | I | IV_4^6 | I | V_6 | I | IV_6 | I_4^6 V_7 | I ‖

6. $\frac{3}{4}$ | I | IV_6 | V_6 | I | V_3^4 | I_6 | II_6 V_7 | I ‖

60

Continuation of a Given Motive

The following procedure is recommended for learning to improvise in this fashion:

1. Complete the first phrase by adding two measures to the given two measures.

    a. Decide upon the harmonic content of these two new measures; establish a cadence that gives a feeling of incompleteness.

    b. Play the left-hand part only, maintaining the style given in the first two measures.

    c. In the right hand add a melody that continues the style of the given melody and that cadences in such a way as to invite a second phrase.

2. Add a second phrase of four measures to complete the period form.

    a. Decide upon the harmonic content of these four measures. Make sure that this second phrase joins well to the first phrase and that it closes with a strong final cadence.

    b. Play the left-hand part only.

    c. In the right hand add a melody that balances with that of the first phrase and that ends with a feeling of finality.

3. Play the entire period.

A possible solution of No. 1 in the following assignment might be:

1. Completion of the first phrase.

    a. Harmonic content of the next two measures:

$$\overset{\text{given}}{\overbrace{\text{I} \quad | \quad \text{V}^4_3}} \quad | \quad \text{V}^6_5 \quad | \quad \text{I} \quad |$$

    b. Left hand only:

c. Added melody:

2. Second phrase of four measures.

  a. Harmonic content:

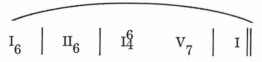

$$\text{I}_6 \quad | \quad \text{II}_6 \quad | \quad \text{I}_4^6 \quad \text{V}_7 \quad | \quad \text{I} \, \|$$

  b. Left hand only:

  c. Added melody:

Assignment 9.   Continue the following motives into period form, using the procedure outlined above.

1. Allegro

2. Grazioso

3. Allegretto

FOUR-PART HARMONIZATION

When a continuo part is realized, the solo line is <u>not</u> played on the keyboard instrument. But when a given melody (such as a hymn or similar piece) is harmonized in four-part vocal style, the melody (or soprano) line <u>is</u> played as the top voice. This kind of music is intended to be sung in four-part harmony. The piano serves merely as a substitute for or reinforcement of the four vocal parts.

The procedure is the same as for the harmonization of a figured bass, except that the melodic line is also given. With an unfigured bass, root position or any appropriate inversion may be used; the performer must determine which member of the chord is in the lowest voice.

<u>Assignment 10.</u> Harmonize the following in four-part vocal style, playing the soprano and bass as given and adding the alto and tenor voices. Then transpose them to other keys.

1. Giardini, "Come, Thou Almighty King"

2. Haydn, "O Worship the King"

3. Abridged from a chorale by C. Kocher

4. Haydn, "The Spacious Firmament on High"

OTHER STYLES

Inversions of chords used for neighboring and passing motion lend themselves well to all styles of accompaniment patterns. Here, as in the Alberti style, the bass line should form good counterpoint to the melody.

<u>Assignment 11.</u>   Accompany the following melodies in appropriate styles.

Bohemian

A. Thomas, *Mignon*, "Gavotte"

Gounod, *Faust*, "Waltz"

Assignment 12. Continue the accompaniments of the following in the styles of the composers.

Beethoven, *Sonata*, Op. 49, No. 2

2. Andante grazioso — Mozart, Viennese Sonatina IV*

IMPROVISATION

Assignment 13. Over the following harmonic pattern, continue the left hand in the given style. Add a melody in the right hand in habanera style.

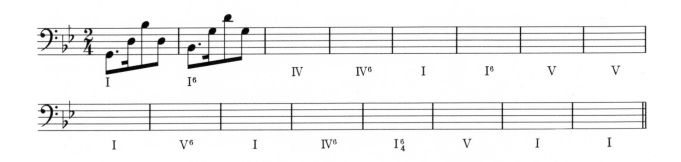

Assignment 14. Over the harmonic patterns given on page 60, improvise in styles other than Alberti.

*By permission of the publisher, taken from Hinrichsen Edition, No. 12; Sole agents: C. F. Peters Corporation, 373 Park Avenue South, N.Y., N.Y., 10016.

Assignment 15. Continue the following into period form, using representative vocabulary. Plan the entire harmonic structure carefully before beginning to play.

1. Allegro — Mozart, *Viennese Sonatina I**
p grazioso

2. Allegro con brio — Beethoven, *Piano Concerto I,* Op. 15 (Original in C major)
mf

*By permission of the publisher, taken from Hinrichsen Edition, No. 12; Sole agents: C. F. Peters Corporation, 373 Park Avenue South, N.Y., N.Y., 10016.

Chapter Six

THE SUBMEDIANT TRIAD

Compare the following harmonizations of the first phrase of "America."

EXAMPLE 1a.

EXAMPLE 1b.

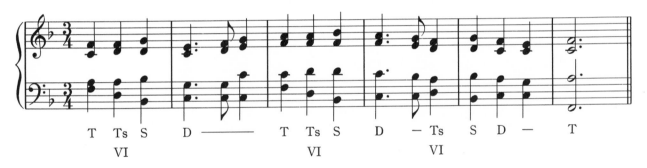

Notice that the triad on VI serves in each case as a substitute for the tonic chord which it replaces, in the same way that II_6 substitutes for IV. Notice also that VI (D F A) is a minor triad substituting for I (F A C), a major triad.

This opening phrase of "America" illustrates two of the best uses of the submediant triad. In the first and third measures, VI on the second beat avoids the repetition of the tonic triad. This downward movement by thirds makes an interesting bass line and creates a strong harmonic progression.

In the fourth measure where one would expect a cadence, the triad VI is used on the third beat instead of I, thus stretching the phrase into six measures. When an expected V_7 I, or authentic cadence at the end of a phrase is replaced by V_7 VI, we have the most used type of deceptive or interrupted cadence.

In the minor mode the submediant chord is a major triad in contrast to the minor tonic. When going from V to VI, or VI to V, it is necessary to double the third in VI in order to avoid the leap of an augmented second.

EXAMPLE 2.

Assignment 1.   Play Examples 1 and 2 in other keys.

Assignment 2.   Study and transpose the following progressions.

EXAMPLE 3.

(a)

(b)

(c)

EXAMPLE 4.

After playing Example 4 in several keys, improvise different melodies above it in the right hand.

FIGURED BASSES AND CONTINUOS

<u>Assignment 3.</u>   Harmonize the following figured basses.

<u>Assignment 4.</u>   Realize the following continuos.

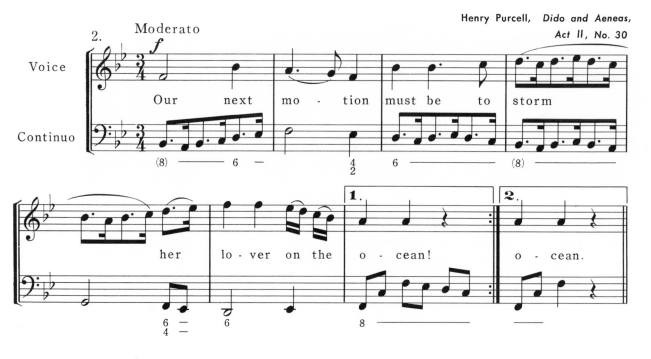

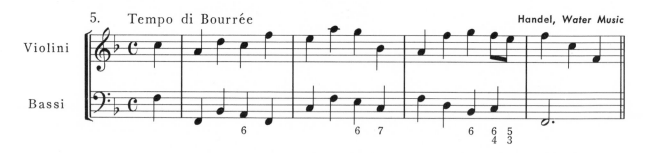

ACCOMPANIMENTS

Assignment 5.   Accompany the following melody in the style used by the composer.

Assignment 6.   Accompany the following melodies in appropriate styles.

Assignment 7. Play by ear accompaniments to the following familiar songs:

1. Home, Sweet Home
2. Old Man River
3. Sourwood Mountain
4. Swing Low, Sweet Chariot
5. Vive la Compagnie (Vive l' Amour, or Let Every Good
   Fellow Now Join in the Song)

FOUR-PART HARMONIZATION

Assignment 8. Harmonize the following in four-part vocal style, playing the
soprano and bass as given and adding the alto and tenor voices.
Then transpose them to other keys.

Carey, "America"

"Auld Lang Syne"

Assignment 9.　Over the following harmonic patterns, improvise melodies and accompaniments in various styles, keys, and meters, in both the major and minor modes.

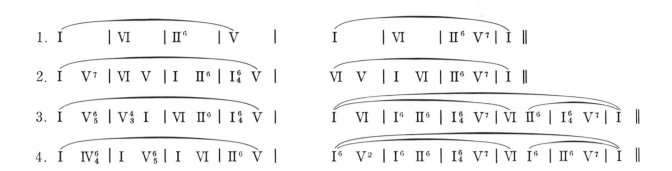

1. I $\quad$ | VI $\quad$ | II^6 $\quad$ | V $\quad$ | $\quad$ I $\quad$ | VI $\quad$ | II^6 V^7 | I ‖

2. I $\,$ V^7 | VI V | I $\,$ II^6 | I$^6_4$ V | $\quad$ VI $\,$ V | I $\,$ VI | II^6 V^7 | I ‖

3. I $\,$ V$^6_5$ | V$^4_3$ I | VI II^6 | I$^6_4$ V | $\quad$ I $\,$ VI | I^6 $\,$ II^6 | I$^6_4$ V^7 | VI $\,$ II^6 | I$^6_4$ V^7 | I ‖

4. I $\,$ IV$^6_4$ | I $\,$ V$^6_5$ | I $\,$ VI | II^6 V | $\quad$ I^6 $\,$ V^2 | I^6 $\,$ II^6 | I$^6_4$ V^7 | VI $\,$ I^6 | II^6 V^7 | I ‖

Assignment 10.　Extend the following into period form, using representative vocabulary.　Plan the entire harmonic structure carefully before beginning to play.

1.　Giocoso

2.　Allegretto

3.　Adagio piangevole

Chapter Seven

THE MEDIANT TRIAD

This, the least used of the diatonic triads, is found frequently in sequences and in descending scale harmonizations. (See Chapter 13, Examples 2b, d, e, f, g, h). The mediant triad may be heard as dominant function (especially when used in first inversion or when preceded by V), or as tonic function (especially when preceded by I).

EXAMPLE 1.

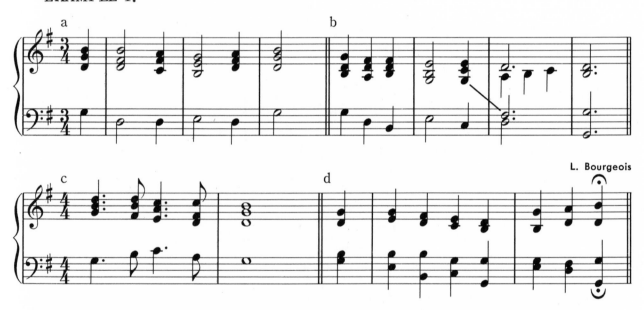

L. Bourgeois

In the minor mode, III is an augmented triad when used as dominant function. In its more frequent use as tonic substitute, however, it is a major triad.

EXAMPLE 2.

Assignment 1. Play the progressions of Examples 1 and 2 in other keys.

Assignment 2. Harmonize the following figured basses:

Assignment 3. Realize the following continuos.

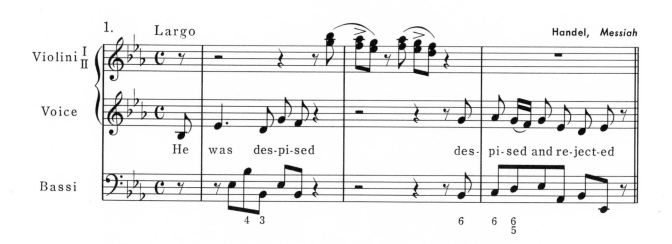

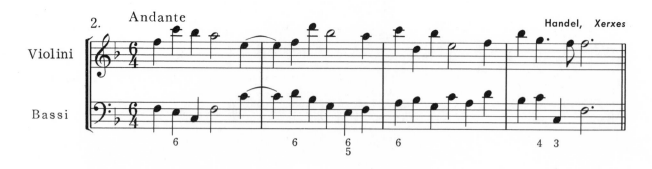

Assignment 4.   Accompany the following melodies in appropriate styles.

Tempo di Valzer lento — Puccini, *La Boheme*, "Musetta's Waltz"

Tempo di Marcia — Tchaikovsky, *Nutcracker Suite*, "March"

<u>Assignment 5.</u>   Play by ear accompaniments to the following familiar songs:

1. Cantique de Noel (O Holy Night) chorus
2. Over the Rainbow
3. Reuben and Rachel
4. Sweet Betsy from Pike

Chapter Eight

THE AEOLIAN AND DORIAN MODES

Many melodies are harmonized wholly or in part in modes other than major or minor. Harmonization of the medieval modes is a special study in itself, but the unique flavor of many melodies can be retained by simple adjustments of the minor mode. The use of the subtonic (major VII), the minor dominant, and the major mediant enables one to harmonize melodies in the Aeolian mode (natural minor).

EXAMPLE 1.

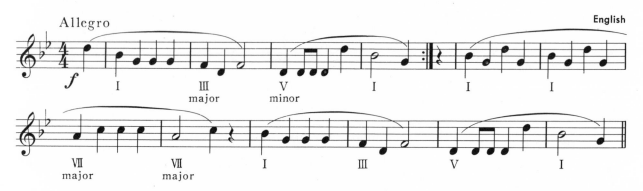

Many folk melodies are in the Dorian mode.

When the B-natural must be harmonized, a major IV or minor II will be needed. But this mode may also use a B-flat; it is then harmonized in the same way as the Aeolian mode.

EXAMPLE 2.

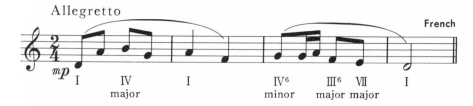

The following are characteristic progressions.

EXAMPLE 3.

Assignment 1. Transpose the progressions of Example 3.

Assignment 2. Harmonize the following figured basses.

Assignment 3. Realize the following continuo.

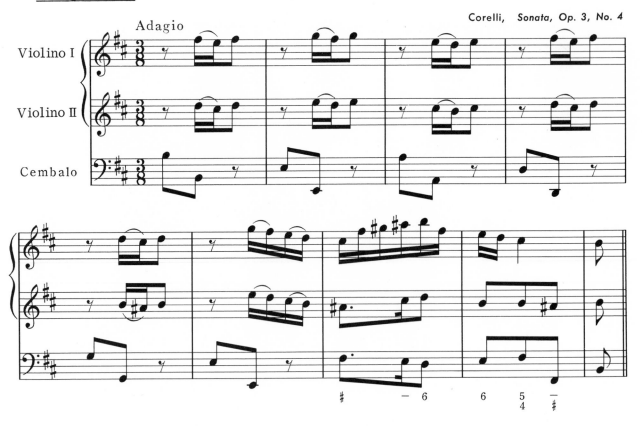

Assignment 4. Accompany the following melodies in appropriate styles.

Chapter Nine

THE LEADING-TONE TRIAD

The triad on the leading tone is used almost exclusively in the first inversion. It functions essentially as neighboring or passing motion.

EXAMPLE 1.

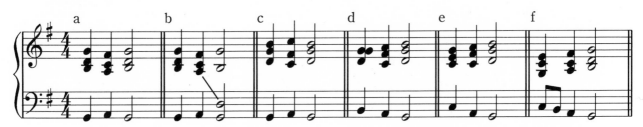

Although this chord is found in piano accompaniments, its more practical use is in four-part harmony.

Assignment 1.   Transpose the progressions of Example 1 to other keys.

Assignment 2.   Realize the following continuos.

Chapter Ten

SUCCESSIVE CHORDS OF THE SIXTH

A technique frequently used by composers is the harmonization of a passage with consecutive parallel chords of the sixth. This device is often referred to as fauxbourdon.

In its original meaning, fauxbourdon was a fifteenth-century Burgundian technique in which a given melody was enriched by the addition of voices a fourth and a sixth below it. This device has continued to be used by composers to the present day. When applied to "America," the result would be:

EXAMPLE 1.

Observe that, except for the first and last chords, all voices move in parallel motion, and that this entire phrase can be seen as nothing but passing and neighboring motion around the tonic chord.

It was customary in the seventeenth and eighteenth centuries to play continuo passages using three or more consecutive sixths or their variants (successive 7-6, 7-6 or 5-6, 5-6 figurations) in three-part harmony, with the sixth above the bass at the top of the chord to escape parallel fifths. This avoided the rather clumsy voice leading which would result if such passages were done in four-part harmony. The remainder of the continuo passages which did not involve such consecutive sixths were, however, generally done in four parts. *

The following is a practical realization of such a continuo passage.

---

*For a more complete discussion of this matter, see Arnold, F. T. The Art of Accompaniment from a Thorough-bass (London: Oxford University Press, 1931), and Bach, C. P. E. Essay On the True Art of Playing Keyboard Instruments, trans. by W. J. Mitchell (New York: W. W. Norton & Company, Inc., 1948).

EXAMPLE 2.

Adagio

Corelli, *Sonata, Op. 3, No. 2*

Violino I

Violino II

Organo

Assignment 1.   Realize the following continuos.

1.   Allegro

Corelli, *Sonata, Op. 5, No. 1*

Violino

Cembalo

2.   Vivace

Corelli, *Sonata, Op. 3, No. 1*

Violini I
       II

Cembalo

Corelli,　Concerto Grosso, Op. 6 , No. 10

3.

Allegro

Violin I

Violin II

Cembalo

4.

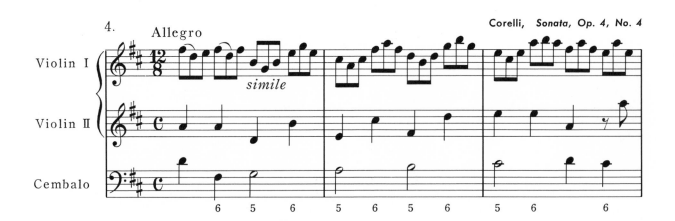

5.

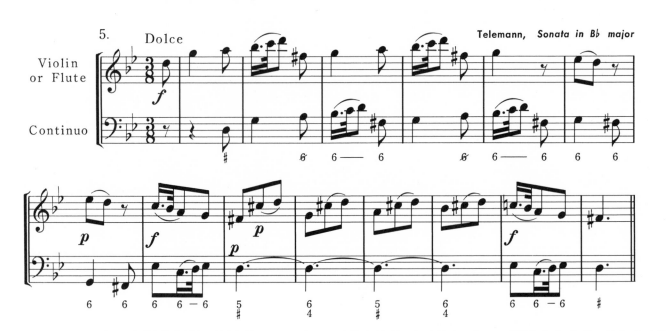

Telemann, *Sonata in B♭ major*

Assignment 3. Over the following harmonic patterns, improvise melodies and accompaniments in various styles, keys, and meters, in both major and minor. In the minor mode, use the natural form of the scale except at cadences.

I V_3^4 | V_5^6 I | II_6 VI | V_7 V_2 | I_6 II_6 | III_6 IV_6 | I_4^6 V_7 | I ‖

I V_6 | IV_6 III_6 | II_6 I_6 | V V_6 | VI_6 V_6 | IV_6 III_6 | II_6 V_7 | I ‖

I VII_6 | VI_6 V_6 | IV_6 III_6 | II_6 V | I V_6 | VI III_6 | IV I_6 | V_7 I ‖

I_6 IV | VII_6 III | VI_6 II | V | I VII_6 | VI_6 V_6 | IV_6 V_7 | I ‖

I_6 VI_6 | VII_6 V_6 | VI_6 IV_6 | I_4^6 V | IV_6 II_6 | III_6 I_6 | II_6 V_7 | I ‖

Chapter Eleven

THE SUPERTONIC SEVENTH CHORD AND ITS INVERSIONS

The supertonic seventh chord contains all the tones of the triads on IV and II. It thus has strong subdominant function.

When the dominant seventh chord resolves to the tonic, the root movement is down a fifth (or up a fourth). This same kind of root movement (often called <u>cadencing resolution</u>) is found when the supertonic chord resolves to the dominant.

It is conservative practice to prepare the seventh of II_7, that is, to have it in the same voice in the preceding chord. When the II_7 resolves to V or V_7 (its most common resolution), the seventh of II_7 moves down a degree to the third of the dominant chord.

The first inversion of this chord ($II\,{}^6_5$) is the one most frequently used, but the root position (II_7) and the third inversion (II_2) are also often found. Less often encountered, however, is the second inversion ($II\,{}^4_3$). Frequently, the third inversion is found at the beginning of a theme in the progression I II_2 V ${}^6_5$ (or V_6) I.

EXAMPLE 1.

In four-part harmony, when the sevenths of both II_7 and V_7 are prepared and both chords are in root position, the fifth is omitted in one chord or the other. In some instances, both chords may be incomplete.

EXAMPLE 2.

Because the supertonic seventh chord is a combination of the tones of IV and II, it is sometimes used as a IV chord with an added neighboring or passing sixth, resolving to a tonic chord.

EXAMPLE 3.

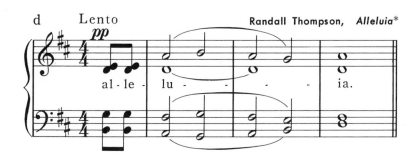

Assignment 1. Transpose the progressions of Examples 1 and 2 to other keys, both major and minor.

Assignment 2. Harmonize the following figured basses.

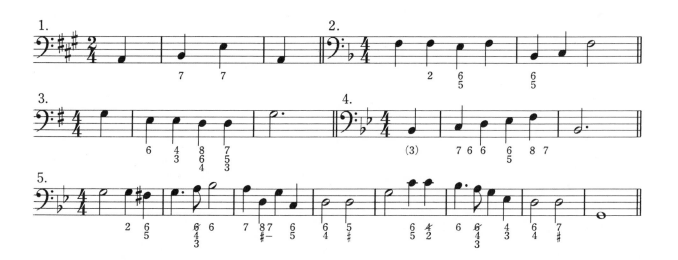

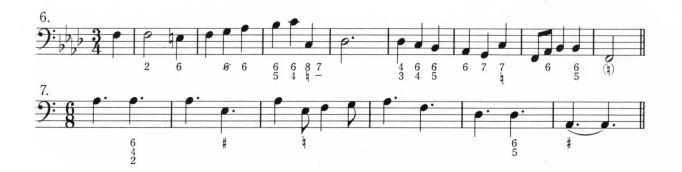

6.

7.

Assignment 3. Realize the following continuos.

1. Grave — Corelli, *Sonata, Op. 5, No. 2*

Violino

Cembalo

2. Tempo di Minuetto — Handel, *Water Music*

Violini

Bassi

3. Vivace — Corelli, *Sonata, Op. 3, No. 1*

Violino I

Violino II

Organo

4. J. S. Bach, *Geistliche Lied*

Voice / Continuo

Auf, auf! mein Herz, mit Freud - en gen Him - mel ist ge - reist.

5. Affettuoso Handel, *Sonata, Op. 1, No. 13*

Violin / Bass

6. J. S. Bach, *Geistliche Lied*

Voice / Continuo

Dir, dir Je - ho - vah will ich sin - gen so wie es dich ge - fäl - lig ist.

Assignment 4. Accompany the following melodies in appropriate styles.

IMPROVISATION

Assignment 5. Extend the following into period form, using as many different inversions of II_7 as possible.

Chapter Twelve

THE REMAINING DIATONIC SEVENTH CHORDS

The remaining diatonic seventh chords are rarely necessary in providing piano accompaniments to melodies, but eighteenth-century continuos often contain chord progressions in cadencing resolutions using some or all of these chords. In Example 1, note that the sevenths are prepared, and that in root position the fifth of every other seventh chord must be omitted in order to avoid faulty voice leading.

EXAMPLE 1.

The diminished seventh chord (VII_7 in the minor mode) is the most used of all these chords and is found in all inversions.

EXAMPLE 2.

The progression IV_7 to V is sometimes found at cadences. When the third or fifth of IV_7 is in the top voice, this progression presents no problem (Example 3 a, b). But when the seventh of IV_7 is at the top, the fifth of V must be doubled in order to avoid parallel fifths (Example 3 c, d, e).

EXAMPLE 3.

Assignment 1.   Transpose the progressions in Examples 1, 2, and 3 to other keys.

Assignment 2.   Realize the following continuos.

Corelli, Sonata, Op. 2, No. 7

Chapter Thirteen

MELODIES HARMONIZED WHOLLY OR IN PART
WITH A CHORD TO EACH NOTE

One of the differences between instrumental and four-part vocal style lies in the speed of chord change, with the instrumental style generally using fewer chords per measure.

The melodies studied thus far have been of the instrumental type, with very few places demanding a chord change on successive melody notes. Example 1a shows "Long Long Ago" arranged with the kind of piano accompaniment it might have been given had this melody been used in Chapter 5.

EXAMPLE 1a.

In Example 1b the same piece is arranged for four voices. Because everyone sings the same words, there is a chord under every melody note, and there are more chord changes than there were in Example 1a. Basically, however, the first two measures are still tonic, and the dominant and subdominant chords in measures 1 and 2, which are necessary to a satisfactory vocal-style setting, are passing or neighboring chords. The tonic chord in measure 3 is also an ornamenting chord.

EXAMPLE 1b.

Three things will aid in accompanying melodies in four-part vocal style:

1. Mastery of the four-part examples given in the preceding chapters.

2. Awareness that the typical phrase moves in an order of T S D T chords but with ornamenting harmonies interspersed among the functional chords.

3. A knowledge of some good harmonizations of the complete ascending and descending scales, and of idiomatic progressions involving parts of the scale.

Assignment 1. Play the following in all major and minor keys, and in various rhythms:

SCALE HARMONIZATIONS

EXAMPLE 2.

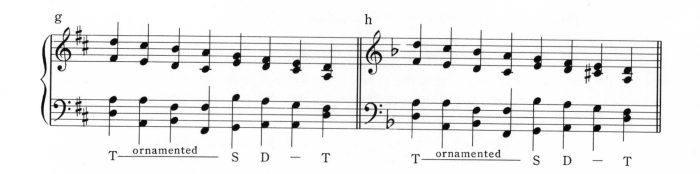

IDIOMS

EXAMPLE 3.

The following folk melody lends itself well to four-part vocal style, and can be harmonized by using only portions of the scales shown in Example 2.

EXAMPLE 4.

For the first four measures, use the beginning and ending of the scale harmonization shown in Example 2a and b; for the second four measures, use the same chords in the key of A major. This harmonization works well because the first four melody notes of each phrase require tonic function, and the last four notes, as the cadence, require subdominant, dominant, tonic.

The third phrase (measures 9-12) will sound well with any descending scale harmonization which is basically an elaboration of the tonic chords, as Example 2e. The harmonization of the fourth phrase can be almost the same as that of the first phrase.

Assignment 2.   Harmonize the following melodies in four-part vocal style.

In harmonizing a melody in four parts at the piano, the ideal is, of course, to have perfect voice leading. In writing such a harmonization, one may take ample time to work out all details. In playing, however, especially at sight, it is better to maintain the rhythmic flow and the spirit of the music, even at the cost of occasional "slips from grace." Many folk melodies which lend themselves well to four-part harmonization contain some places which prove difficult to handle fluently in a strict style.

EXAMPLE 5.

Both of these melodies can be harmonized without errors in voice leading, but for playing at the piano the style shown above is more practical.

Assignment 3.   Accompany the following melodies in essentially four-part vocal style. Let your goal be maintenance of tempo, rhythm, and the character of the music.

Chapter 5, Assignment 7, No. 6; Assignment 11, Nos. 2, 3.

Chapter 6, Assignment 6, Nos. 4, 5, 8.

Chapter 7, Assignment 4, Nos. 1, 2.

In many compositions the composer may use two, three, four, five, six, or even more parts as fits his needs. It is not a matter, here, of real four-part vocal writing. The effect is that of a melody supported by harmonic background. An inner voice may even double the melody at the octave.

EXAMPLE 6.

Accompany the following melodies, varying the number of voices as seems appropriate.

Sometimes instrumental and four-part vocal styles are mixed within a single phrase. The opening melody of Beethoven's Symphony No. 8 could be harmonized thus:

EXAMPLE 7.

a   Allegro vivace

or thus:

b   Allegro vivace

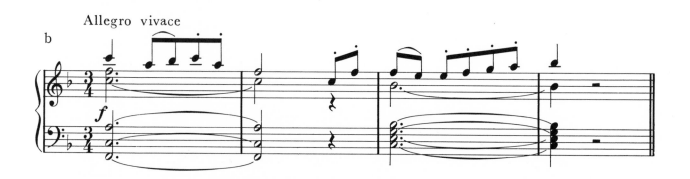

What Beethoven actually wrote, however, is:

c   Allegro vivace

As one can readily see, the passing <u>tones</u> of measure 3 in Example 7 a and b are replaced in the four-part harmony of Example 7c by passing <u>chords</u>. While many melodies, like the Beethoven excerpt, can be harmonized in a purely instrumental style, as in Example 7a and b, they are more satisfactory with a mixture of styles, as in Example 7c.

116

Because harmonies tend to change faster at cadences than in the course of a phrase, an instrumental-style accompaniment frequently changes to a more harmonic style at cadence points.

EXAMPLE 8.

Mozart, Sonata, K. 284
(adapted)

The possibilities for various treatments of these styles are so nearly limitless that only an introduction to this kind of playing can be given here. Students are urged to use their taste and imagination in providing this kind of accompaniment.

Assignment 5.   Accompany the following melodies in an appropriate combination of styles.

Chapter Fourteen

SECONDARY DOMINANTS OF V

EXAMPLE 1.

The chords of Example 1 seem to be in the key of E major, but when they are placed within the entire phrase from which they were taken,

EXAMPLE 2.

they have a somewhat different function. The phrase is clearly in the key of A major and the chord at the asterisk cannot be $V\frac{4}{3}$ in the key of E major, but instead is the dominant of the E chord, which is V in the key of A major. Heard in isolation, the chord at the asterisk makes the E major chord a tonic. Heard in context, it merely strengthens the dominant function of the E major chord, which has been made more prominent because it has been preceded by its own dominant. This E major chord might be said to have been briefly "tonicized," [*] and the "$V\frac{4}{3}$ of" referred to as a secondary dominant.

Since any major or minor triad can, under proper conditions, function as a tonic chord, any major or minor triad may be preceded by its own dominant. Secondary dominants may be used in any inversion.

[*] Roger Sessions, Harmonic Practice (New York: Harcourt, Brace & World, Inc., 1951), Chapter 8.

EXAMPLE 3.

Assignment 1.   Transpose the progressions of Example 3 to other keys.   Play
parts a, c, d, e, and g in minor as well as major.

Assignment 2.   Realize the following continuos.

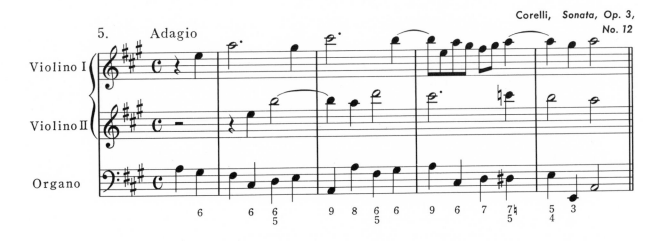

Corelli, *Sonata, Op. 3, No. 12*

Assignment 3. Continue the following accompaniments in the styles used by the composers. In order to locate appropriate places for the dominant of V, first find where the melody demands a V chord; then examine the preceding notes to see if they will invite a secondary dominant.

Beethoven, *Sonata, Op. 2, No. 2*

Schumann, *Slumber Song,*
Op. 124

2. Allegretto

Assignment 4. Accompany the following melodies in appropriate styles.

Moderato

German

1. *p*   *cresc.*

Presto

Italian

2. *f*

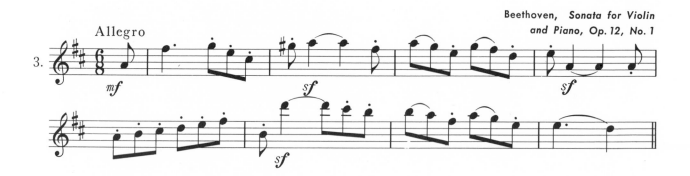

Beethoven, *Sonata for Violin
and Piano, Op. 12, No. 1*

Allegro

3. *mf*   *sf*   *sf*

sf

FAMILIAR SONGS

Assignment 5.   Play by ear accompaniments to the following familiar songs:

1.   All Through the Night
2.   Bicycle Built for Two (Daisy Bell)
3.   Caisson Song (Field Artillery March)
4.   Carry Me Back to Old Virginny
5.   Colonel Bogey
6.   Jingle Bells
7.   My Old Kentucky Home
8.   Our Boys Will Shine Tonight
9.   Over There
10.   Pop Goes the Weasel
11.   Turkey in the Straw (Old Zip Coon)

Chapter Fifteen

SECONDARY DOMINANTS OF IV

In the major mode the V_7 of IV is spelled as if it were the tonic seventh with lowered seventh. In the minor mode the third of V_7 of IV must be raised to make the triad major. This secondary dominant is used to intensify the subdominant chord to which it leads.

EXAMPLE 1.

V_7 of V may resolve directly to V_7 of the key; this V_7 in turn may resolve, not to I, but to V_7 of IV. Such a progression creates a sequential chain of chords, each of which is the dominant of the next.

EXAMPLE 2.

Assignment 1.   Transpose the progressions of Examples 1 and 2 to other keys.

Assignment 2.   Realize the following continuos.

Assignment 3. Continue the following accompaniments in the styles used by the composers.

1. Moderato cantabile molto espressivo

Beethoven, *Sonata, Op. 110*

2. Andante tranquillo

Mendelssohn, *Midsummer Night's Dream, "Nocturne"*

Assignment 4. Accompany the following melodies in appropriate styles. In order to locate places for the dominant of IV, first find where the melody demands a IV chord; then examine the preceding notes to see if they invite a secondary dominant. Some of the following melodies need V_7 of V as well as V_7 of IV.

1.

2.

3.

4.

132

Andante con moto

Edward Purcell, *Passing By*

5.

Tempo di Valse Lento

Schubert, *Waltz, Op. 9b, No. 3*

6.

Brahms, *Der Schmied, Op. 19, No. 4*

Allegro

7.

Scottish

Moderato

8.

Allegro moderato

Haydn, *Trio in E minor*

9.

mf

Andante cantabile

Tchaikovsky, *Romance,*
Op. 5 (adapted)

10.

p dolce

poco piu mosso

mf *rit.*

a

tempo *cresc.*

f

Assignment 5. Harmonize the following in four-part vocal style, playing the
soprano and bass as given and adding the alto and tenor voices.
Then transpose to other keys.

Ward, *"America, The Beautiful"*

134

Assignment 6.   Play by ear accompaniments to the following familiar songs:

1. Believe Me, If All Those Endearing Young Charms
2. The Blue-Tail Fly (Jimmie Crack Corn)
3. For He's a Jolly Good Fellow
4. Gaily the Troubadour
5. Good Night Ladies
6. Red River Valley
7. Yankee Doodle

IMPROVISATION

Assignment 7.   Over the following harmonic patterns, improvise melodies and accompaniments in various styles, keys, and meters, in both major and minor mode.

1. I | V_2 of | IV_6 II_6 | V | I VI | II^6_5 V^6_5 of | V_{4-3} | I ||

2. I II_2 | I V_2 of | V_6 V_7 | VI | V^4_3 of IV | V^6_5 of V V of V^7 | I^6_4 V_7 | I ||

3. I V_6 I | VI V^4_3 of V V_7 | I V_7 of | IV^6_4 V^6_5 | I II_6 I^6_4 V_7 I ||

4. V_2 of | V_6 | V_2 of | IV_6 | I^6_4 | V_2 | I_6 V^4_3 | I ||

135

Chapter Sixteen

SECONDARY DOMINANTS OF II

Because only a major or minor triad may serve as a tonic chord, the supertonic triad may be preceded by its dominant only in the major mode. In the minor mode the supertonic, being a diminished triad, cannot be tonicized. V_7 of II may also resolve to II or II_7 with its third raised.

EXAMPLE 1.

Assignment 1. Transpose the progressions of Example 1 to other keys.

Assignment 2. Realize the following continuo.

Assignment 3. Continue the following accompaniments in the styles used by the composers.

Assignment 4. Accompany the following melodies in appropriate styles.

Assignment 5. Play by ear accompaniments to the following familiar songs:

1. Blow the Man Down
2. La Cucaracha
3. The Sidewalks of New York

Chapter Seventeen

SECONDARY DOMINANTS OF VI

The secondary dominants of the submediant work equally well in both the major and minor modes. They are often found in sequential patterns (Example 1b, c, d) and as passing sonorities between the chords of I VI IV or I VI II$_6$ (Example 1a, e, f).

EXAMPLE 1.

Assignment 1.   Transpose the progressions of Example 1 to other keys.

Assignment 2.   Realize the following continuos.

142

Assignment 3. Accompany the following melodies in appropriate styles.

*Example 1f is a reduction of this passage to four-part harmony.

Andante con moto

"The Old Refrain"

Assignment 4.   Harmonize the following in four-part vocal style, playing the
soprano and bass as given and adding the alto and tenor voices.
Then transpose them to other keys.

J. S. Smith
"The Star-Spangled Banner"

1.

2.

Assignment 5. Play by ear accompaniments to the following familiar songs:

1. Funiculi-Funicula (A Merry Life) chorus
2. Jolly Old Saint Nicholas
3. Love's Old Sweet Song (chorus)
4. Sailing, Sailing, Over the Bounding Main (chorus)
5. Waltzing Mathilda
6. Yankee Doodle-oodle

SUCCESSIVE SECONDARY DOMINANTS

The cadencing progression of successive dominant seventh chords around the circle of fifths is so strong and satisfying that it has long been employed by composers.

EXAMPLE 2.

In such a sequence of secondary dominants, triads often alternate with seventh chords.

EXAMPLE 3.

Assignment 6.   Accompany the following melodies, using successive secondary dominants at the asterisks.

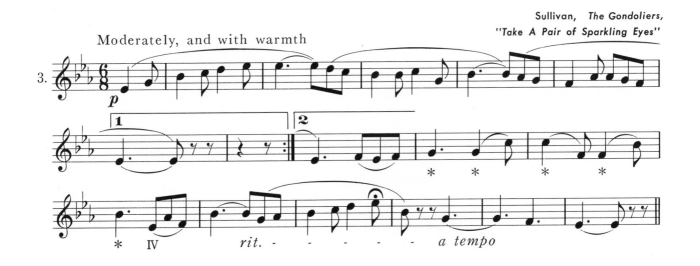

IMPROVISATION

<u>Assignment 7.</u> Extend the following into period form, using secondary dominants.

2. Andantino

ossia più facile

3. Andante con moto

Chapter Eighteen

SECONDARY DOMINANTS OF III AND VII

The secondary dominants of III are found in both modes, but they appear more frequently in the minor mode where they create a momentary feeling of the relative major.

EXAMPLE 1.

Assignment 1.   Transpose the progressions of Example 1 to other keys.

Assignment 2.   Realize the following continuos.

Mendelssohn, *Song Without Words*, Op. 62, No. 5

Schumann, *Album for the Young*, Op. 68, No. 6

The secondary dominants of VII are found only in the minor mode as embellishments of the major triad on the subtonic.

Assignment 4.   Realize the following continuos.

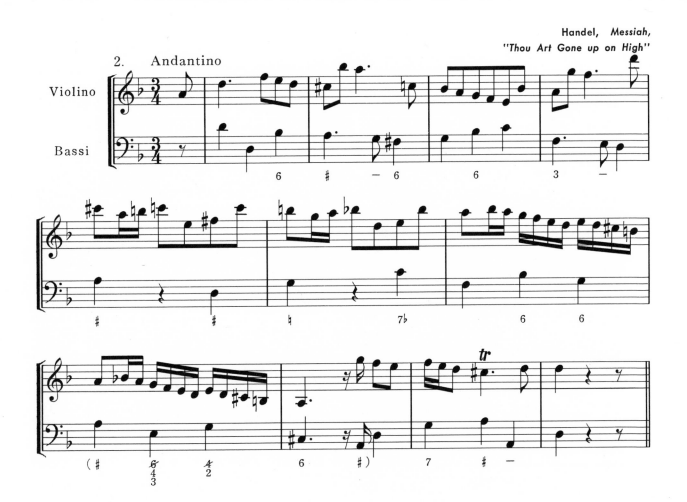

Chapter Nineteen

MODULATION TO THE DOMINANT

For the sake of harmonic interest and clarity of form, a composer almost invariably shifts the tonal center within the course of any larger composition. This shift of key center is called <u>modulation.</u> The first key center must be well established before effecting a change, and the new key must be confirmed by means of a definite cadence in that key.

Play Example 1a, listening to it carefully. Then analyze the chords in the key in which the excerpt seems to be.

EXAMPLE 1a.

Now play Example 1b. This is the entire theme, of which Example 1a is only the second phrase.

EXAMPLE 1b.

156

Observe the tonal variety which Haydn obtains by shifting briefly to the key of A major in the second phrase, instead of remaining in the key of D major for the entire theme. This situation is typical of many compositions.

Note, in the fifth measure, that the A major chord (first inversion) would sound as if it were clearly V_6 in the key of D if one stopped at this point; on the other hand, it sounds clearly as if it were I_6 in the key of A if one begins at this point, as in Example 1a. Instead of moving directly from the first key to the new one, the composer usually passes through one or more chords belonging to both keys before establishing the new key by means of a cadence. Such a chord (or chords) is known as the "common" or "pivot" chord(s), and it must function clearly in both keys.

Heard by itself, Example 1a clearly consists of T S D T chords in the key of A major. But when heard in context, as the second phrase of a rounded binary form in the key of D major, Example 1a, while still a unit in the key of A major, is really an emphasis or prolongation of V in the key of D major.

Some musicians may prefer to analyze the second phrase of Example 1b as all in D major with a tonicization of V. The answer to this is that tonicization and modulation are essentially the same process, differing only in length or degree of strength. There must be a meeting point, and so there must also be borderline cases which one authority would classify one way, another the other way.

However, there are many harmonic patterns, such as $I_{(6)}$ II_6 ($I{}^{6}_{4}$) V_7 I, which occur over and over in music, and which the mind grasps as a sort of cadential unit of musical thought. Therefore, when the new key is reinforced by a cadential formula, most authorities agree that in such music as Example 1b, the second phrase should be I_6 II_6 $I{}^{6}_{4}$ V_7 I in the key of A major. The E minor chord in measure ten and the G major chord in measure eighteen, however, have merely been preceded by their own dominants, and these keys (E minor and G major) have not been established by means of a cadence. These two chords are tonicized only lightly, whereas the A major chord of the second phrase has been tonicized strongly.

Assignment 1.   Realize the following continuos.

4. Allegro

Corelli, *Sonata, Op. 2, No. 1*

Violino I

Violino II

Cembalo

Assignment 2. Play accompaniments to the following melodies. First find the phrase that cadences in the dominant key. Work back from that cadence as far as possible in the dominant key and locate the common chord. Then complete the harmonization of the entire melody. The first five melodies lend themselves to four-part style harmonization; the others, to various instrumental styles.

Assignment 3. Harmonize the following in four-part vocal style. Then transpose them to other keys.

Play by ear accompaniments to the following familiar songs:

1.   The Ash Grove
2.   Au Clair de la Lune
3.   The Blue Bells of Scotland
4.   Flow Gently, Sweet Afton
5.   Hark! the Herald Angels Sing
6.   Jeanie with the Light Brown Hair
7.   The Loreley
8.   O Come, All Ye Faithful
9.   Thanksgiving Hymn (We Gather Together)

IMPROVISATION

Assignment 5.   Extend each of the following into a period, closing the second
phrase with a strong cadence in the dominant key. After this
one period is perfect, enlarge the form into a rounded binary,
such as shown in Example 1b. The third phrase must lead back
to the original key, and in the return of the first period, the
second phrase must close in the tonic key. Think out the entire
harmonic pattern carefully before beginning to play.

Chapter Twenty

MODULATION TO THE RELATIVE MAJOR

When a composition is in the major mode, the most common modulation is to the key of the dominant. But when a composition is in the minor mode, the modulation is frequently to the key of the relative major.

EXAMPLE 1.

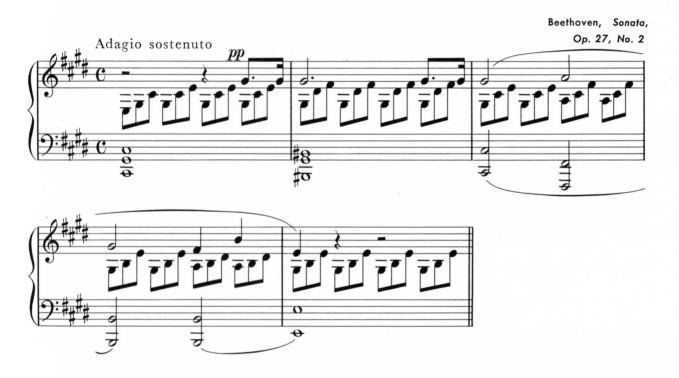

Beethoven, *Sonata,*
Op. 27, No. 2

Adagio sostenuto

Assignment 1. Accompany the following melodies.

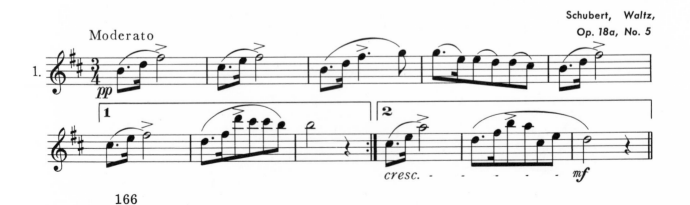

Schubert, *Waltz,*
Op. 18a, No. 5

Moderato

1.

Because a minor key and its relative major are so closely related, it is not unusual to move directly from one key to another. Such a progression may be considered a tonicization of the III chord.

EXAMPLE 2.

Assignment 2. Accompany the following melodies.

*By permission of Hug & Co., Zürich: from Easy Compositions from Three Centuries, edited by Kurt Hermann.

169

Assignment 3.   Play by ear accompaniments to the following familiar songs.

        1. We Three Kings of Orient Are
        2. When Johnny Comes Marching Home

Assignment 4.   Realize the following continuos.

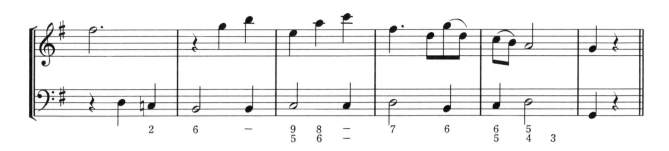

Tartini, *Sonata,* ("The Devil's Trill")

Corelli, *Sonata, Op. 1, No. 10*

Assignment 5. Continue the accompaniment to the following melody in the style used by the composer. Use only single notes in the left hand to outline the harmonies and to add melodic interest.

Handel, Gavotte

Chapter Twenty-one

MODULATION TO THE RELATIVE MINOR

Compositions in the major mode may modulate to the relative minor, either establishing the new key by a definite cadence, or merely passing through it (tonicization).

Assignment 1.   Accompany the following melodies.

Grazioso

4.

5. Allegro

English

Assignment 2. Realize the following continuos.

1. Largo

Corelli, *Sonata, Op. 5, No. 10*

Violino

Cembalo

<table>
</table>

IMPROVISATION

Assignment 3. Extend each of the following into a period, closing the second phrase with a strong cadence in the key of the relative minor. After the first period is perfect, enlarge the form into a rounded binary, following the directions given in Chapter 19, page 165.

1. Allegretto

2. Allegro

3. Adagio

Mozart, Viennese Sonatina I*

*By permission of the publisher, taken from Hinrichsen Edition, No. 12; Sole
Agents: C. F. Peters Corporation, 373 Park Avenue South, N. Y., N. Y. 10016.

Chapter Twenty-two

MODULATION FROM MAJOR TO THE MEDIANT MINOR

Instead of modulating to the key of the dominant, compositions in the major mode sometimes modulate to the relative minor of the dominant, thus providing a change of both tonality and modality.

<u>Assignment 1.</u>   Accompany the following melodies.

Brahms, *Waltz, Op. 39, No. 15*

Assignment 2. Continue the accompaniment to the following melody in the style used by the composer. Either play the melody in the right hand and the full accompaniment in the left hand, or play only the octaves in the left hand and the rest of the accompaniment in the right hand, while a classmate plays the melody on the cello or the violin.

Mendelssohn, *Song Without Words, for Cello, Op. 109*

Assignment 3. Realize the following continuos.

Vivaldi, *Concerto in C Major*

Handel, Rinaldo, *"Lascia ch'io Pianga"*

La - scia ch'io pian - ga mia cru - da sor - te

e che so - spiri la li - ber - tà. e che so -

spi - ri e che so - spiri la li - ber - tà.

Las - cia ch'io pian - ga   mia cru - da sor - te   e che so -
spi - ri la li - ber - tà.   Il duolo in - fran - ga
ques - te ri - tor - te   de' miei mar - ti - ri sol per pie -
tà, de' miei mar - ti - ri sol per pie - tà.

Fine

D.C. al Fine

Chapter Twenty-three

MODULATION TO OTHER CLOSELY RELATED KEYS

The most common modulations are to tonal centers not more than one signature remove away from the key of the composition as a whole. The preceding four chapters have dealt with those modulations most frequently encountered among these key relationships. The following melodies and continuos include the remaining of these modulations.

<u>Assignment 1.</u>   Accompany the following melodies.

J. S. Bach, *Chorale,*
"Ich dank' dir schon"

Assignment 2.   Realize the following continuos.

J. S. Bach, *Geistliche Lied*

IMPROVISATION

Assignment 3. To the following given phrases, improvise five different second phrases, each modulating to a different one of the five most closely related keys.

188

Assignment 4. Continue the accompaniment to the following melody in the style used by the composer. Observe that the contrasting material consists of two phrases, the first with a strong tonicization of the supertonic key, the second a sequence in the tonic key. In the return of the first theme the second phrase is abbreviated.

Mozart, *Allegro, K. 3*

Assignment 5. For each of the following, compose several second phrases, each modulating to a different closely related key. Then continue the periods into rounded binary forms. In the contrasting section, modulate to (or strongly tonicize) a different related key, using sequence if possible.

1. Andante — Beethoven, *Bagatelle*, Op. 126, No. 3

2. Andante — Purcell, *Ayre*

3. Allegro — W. F. Bach, *Allegro*